MARION
JONES

MARION
JONES

CARL EMERSON
THE CHILD'S WORLD®, INC.

ON THE COVER...

Front cover: Marion waves to the crowd after winning the women's 100-meter race at the 2000 Olympics.
Page 2: Marion holds up the gold medal she won in the women's 200-meter race at the 2000 Olympics.

Published in the United States of America by The Child's World®, Inc.
PO Box 326
Chanhassen, MN 55317-0326
800-599-READ
www.childsworld.com

Product Manager Mary Berendes
Editor Katherine Stevenson
Designer Mary Berendes

Photo Credits
© AFP/CORBIS: cover, 6, 16, 19, 20, 22
© Duomo/CORBIS: 13, 15
© Reuters NewMedia Inc./CORBIS: 2, 9, 10

Library of Congress Cataloging-in-Publication Data
Emerson, Carl.
Marion Jones / by Carl Emerson.
p. cm.
ISBN 1-56766-970-0 (alk. paper)
1. Jones, Marion, 1975– .—Juvenile literature.
2. Runners (Sports)—United States—Biography—Juvenile literature.
3. Women runners—United States—Biography—Juvenile literature.
[1. Jones, Marion, 1975– . 2. Track and field athletes. 3. Women—Biography.
4. Afro-Americans—Biography.] I. Title.
GV1061.15 .E44 2001
796.42'2'092—dc21

00-012258

TABLE OF CONTENTS

LIKE A ROCKET

The **sprinters** were lining up for the finals in the women's 100-meter race in the 2000 Olympics. Marion Jones of the United States paced back and forth near the **starting blocks.** At last, she bent down to get into the blocks. She put her feet in the blocks and lined up her fingers near the starting line. She stared straight down at the track. She took a deep breath. Then she looked along the track to the finish line.

As the race started, Marion sprang from the blocks as if she'd been shot out of a cannon. A couple of seconds into the race, it was clear that none of the other runners had a chance of catching her. She was just too fast. Just 10.75 seconds later, Marion crossed the finish line first. She was .37 seconds faster than the next runner. That might not seem like a lot, but it was the biggest win in that Olympic race since 1952.

Marion had won her first Olympic gold medal! Just a few steps after crossing the finish line, she made a little hop as a big smile burst across her face. When she finally slowed down, she realized that she had made a dream come true. She was so happy, she started to cry.

Marion crosses the finish line to win the women's 100-meter race at the 2000 Olympic Games.

EARLY DREAMS

Marion Jones was born on October 12, 1975, in Los Angeles, California. She was a lively little girl who was faster than any of the other kids in her neighborhood—including the boys. She didn't always know that she wanted to be a track and field athlete. But she always believed that she was something special. When she was five, she watched the wedding of Prince Charles and Lady Diana on television. She asked her mom why Diana walked on a red carpet. Marion's mom told her that the carpet was rolled out for special people. Marion said, "When I go places, why don't they roll it out for me?"

But growing up wasn't always easy for Marion. Her father left the family when she was very young, and her mother remarried. Her stepfather, Ira Toler, died in 1987, when Marion was only 11 years old.

Marion found joy in sports, and she was very good right from the beginning. She had dreams of being one of the best athletes in history. Not only was she a great sprinter, she was an outstanding basketball player, too. When she was in sixth grade, Marion wrote in a school assignment that she was going to run in the 1992 Olympics.

Marion smiles during a news conference in Brussels, Belgium, on August 23, 2000.

MAKING HER OWN WAY

Marion's speed and strength became obvious when she was in high school. During her freshman year, she lost only one race. Inger Miller, who would later be Marion's Olympic teammate, defeated Marion in the 100 meters. Marion is a very determined athlete. For the rest of her high school career, Marion never lost another race. And she hasn't ever lost to Miller again.

Marion was one of the best high school track stars ever. She was the California state champion in the 100 meters and 200 meters for four straight years. She still holds the national high school record in the 200 meters. In 1992, at the age of 16, Marion competed in the Olympic trials in track. She was trying to realize her dream of running in the 1992 Olympics. She missed making the team in the 200 meters by only .07 seconds.

A PROUD ATHLETE

Even though Marion fell short, she was offered a spot as an alternate on the 4 x 100 **relay** team going to the 1992 Olympics. Being an alternate meant that she probably wouldn't get a chance to run in the Olympics. But she would still have a chance to win a medal.

Marion runs to win the 100-meter race at the 2000 Golden League track and field meet in Berlin.

Marion didn't want to win an Olympic medal that way. "I wanted my first gold medal to be something I sweated for," she said. "I didn't want anybody giving me one." Marion decided not to go to the Olympics that year.

CHANGING FOCUS

Most people believed that Marion would go on to a successful college career in track. But she was also a great basketball player. In fact, she was named the High School Player of the Year in 1993. She was also offered a **scholarship** to the University of North Carolina. When she accepted, it meant that she would be concentrating on basketball more than track.

Many people were surprised by her decision, but Marion didn't care. She set out to be the best basketball player she could be. She still competed in track, but her focus was basketball. Her hard work in basketball paid off during her freshman season. North Carolina won the 1994 NCAA championship with Marion as the starting point guard.

As fast as her basketball success came, however, Marion ran into tough times. In 1995, she broke her foot twice. With the 1996 Olympics drawing near, Marion decided to give up basketball and work hard on her track events. She missed the Olympic trials in 1996 because her injury hadn't healed, so she began working toward the 2000 Olympics instead.

Medical personnel tend to Marion after her injury at the 1999 World s Competition.

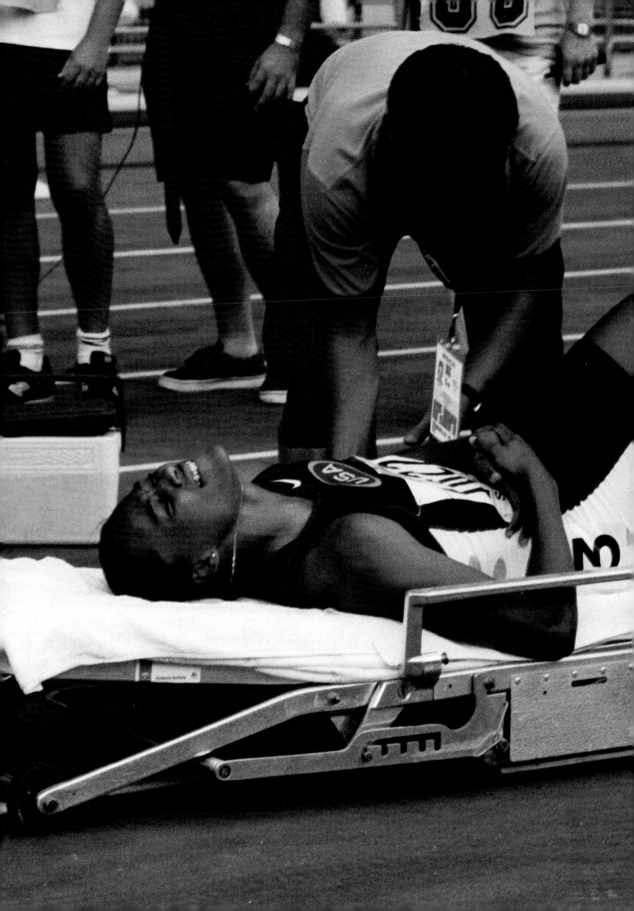

TOUGH TRAINING

Marion has a lot of natural talent, but it takes a great deal of **training** to be a world-class athlete. Marion has to keep her body in top physical condition all the time. She trains six days a week, for five hours each day. She works hard on the track to build her speed and **endurance.** She also works on getting out of the starting blocks quickly. On three of her workout days, she does weight training.

Marion competes in five different events. In three of them she competes on her own: the 100 meters, the 200 meters, and the long jump. In the 4 x 100 and 4 x 400 relay events, she has three teammates. In the 4 x 100, each woman runs 100 meters and passes a baton to the next runner. In the 4 x 400, each woman runs 400 meters.

BACK ON TRACK

Marion's foot finally healed, and she began training seriously for track again. It was 1997—more than three years since she had last competed seriously in track. Many people said that she had been away too long. They thought she wouldn't be able to be a track star again. She would quickly prove them all wrong.

Marion practices how to get out of the starting blocks quickly in 1999.

In 1997, Marion competed in the U. S. Nationals, the nation's most important track meet. In the 100 meters she defeated Gail Devers, the Olympic champion in that event. In the long jump she beat Jackie Joyner-Kersee, another superstar athlete. Marion also won the 100 meters at the World Championships, earning her the title of "World's Fastest Woman."

The next year, she proved she was the top female track athlete in the world. She won 35 of the 36 events in which she competed. She also married C. J. Hunter, who was competing in the shot put at many of the same track meets. In 1999, Marion again won the gold medal in the 100 meters at the World Championships. She also took the bronze medal in the long jump. In the 200 meters, she suffered from back pain and couldn't finish her race.

GREAT EXPECTATIONS

Despite that minor setback, Marion was on top of the world in track. The 2000 Olympics in Sydney, Australia, were drawing nearer. In 1998 Marion set her goal: to win five gold medals in the 2000 Olympics. No woman had ever done that in Olympic track and field. In fact, no Olympic athlete had won five gold medals in track and field since 1924, when a Finnish man named Paavo Nurmi accomplished the feat.

Marion finishes ahead of Gail Devers to win the 100-meter semi-final at the 1999 IAAF World Championships in Athletics.

Marion believed she could do it, and the world began to take notice. As the Olympics approached, newspapers and magazines all over the world were writing stories about her. She was on the cover of dozens of magazines, including *Sports Illustrated* and *Time*. Everyone was talking about whether Marion could really win five gold medals. They were calling it the "Drive for Five."

THE 2000 OLYMPICS

Marion's first event at the Olympics was the 100 meters, her best event. When she won it so easily, she was very excited. But she was also relieved, because the pressure of trying to win her first Olympic gold medal was finally off. It was a great way for her to start. Next was the 200 meters, her second-best event. After all the **qualifying races** were done, Marion was ready for the final. She ran the race in 21.84 seconds and won her second gold medal. It was beginning to look as though Marion might achieve her goal.

Competing in so many events is difficult, because the athletes don't run just one race for each event. Instead, most events have many qualifying races. For example, Marion had to run three qualifying races in the 100 meters and another three in the 200 meters before she could reach the finals. Her job was made even more difficult when reports surfaced that her husband, C. J. Hunter, had used illegal drugs when he competed. Marion did her best to ignore the press reports and prepare for her remaining events.

Marion shouts for joy as she crosses the finish line to win the 100 meters at the 2000 Olympics.

Next up for Marion was the long jump. She faced some serious competition. Each athlete would get six chances to make the jump. In the long jump, the athlete must run down the track and jump from behind a line. Stepping on or over the line is a **foul,** and the jump doesn't count. In third place after five jumps, Marion had one last chance to get the gold medal. Her sixth and final jump looked good, but her foot was on the line. She had fouled. Her dream of winning five gold medals was over—but she did win a bronze medal for third place.

Two of the regular members of the 4 x 100 relay team had injuries and couldn't compete in the Olympics. The four who went to the Olympics, including Marion, had little time to practice together. They finished third, which meant another bronze medal for Marion. However, she finished the Olympics in grand style, helping the 4 x 400 relay team win the gold medal.

LOOKING AHEAD

Marion didn't reach her goal of five Olympic golds. But her total of five medals—three gold and two bronze—in a single Olympics was a new record in women's track. And Marion isn't done. She's already talking about the 2004 Olympics. She has also talked about playing professional basketball in the Women's National Basketball Association (WNBA) someday. "I think the ultimate goal for any athlete is to be considered the greatest ever," she said.

Top photo: Marion hits the sand after an attempt at the long jump in the 2000 Olympics.
Bottom photo: Marion takes off during the women's 4 x 400 relay at the 2000 Olympics.

TIMELINE

October 12, 1975	Marion Jones is born in Los Angeles, California.
1987	Marion's stepfather, Ira Toler, dies.
1990	As a freshman in high school, Marion loses a race to Inger Miller—the only high school race she ever loses.
1992	Marion misses making the Olympic team for the 200 meters by only .07 seconds. She turns down a chance to participate as an alternate on the 4 x 100 relay team.
1993	Marion is named High School Player of the Year in basketball and accepts a scholarship to the University of North Carolina.
1994	North Carolina's basketball team, with Marion as point guard, wins the NCAA championship.
1995	Marion breaks her foot twice.
1997	After returning to track, Marion wins the 100 meters and the long jump at the U. S. Nationals. She also wins the 100 meters at the World Championships.
1998	Marion wins 35 of 36 events in which she competes.
1999	Marion wins the World Championships in the 100 meters.
2000	At the Olympics, Marion wins gold medals in the 100 meters, 200 meters, and 4 x 400 relay. She wins bronze medals in the long jump and 4 x 100 meters.

Marion holds up the U.S. flag after winning the women's 200 meter race at the 2000 Olympics.

GLOSSARY

endurance (en-DUR-ents)
Endurance is the ability to keep going for a long time. Marion Jones trains to improve her endurance.

foul (FOWL)
In the long jump, stepping on or over the jumping line is a foul and makes the jump not count. Marion Jones fouled on her last attempt in the 2000 Olympics.

qualifying races (KWAH-lih-fy-ing RAY-sez)
Qualifying races are run to determine which runners get to race in the finals. Marion Jones had to run several qualifying races before she ran for her Olympic medals.

relay (REE-lay)
A relay race is run by a team of four people, with one person passing a baton to the next. At the 2000 Olympics, Marion Jones competed in two different relays.

scholarship (SKAHL-er-ship)
A scholarship pays part or all of a student's school expenses, often in exchange for playing a sport. Marion Jones received a basketball scholarship to attend the University of North Carolina in 1993.

sprinters (SPRINT-erz)
A sprinter is a track athlete who competes in fast, short-distance races. Marion Jones is a sprinter.

starting blocks (STAR-ting BLOKS)
Starting blocks (often called just "blocks") are sturdy supports that hold a runner's feet at the beginning of a race. Marion Jones and other sprinters push off from the blocks to start running quickly.

training (TRANE-ing)
In sports, training is working out to stay in top physical shape. Marion Jones trains six days a week for five hours each day.

INDEX